Angel Island: The History and Legacy of the Im Francisco Bay

By Charles River Editors

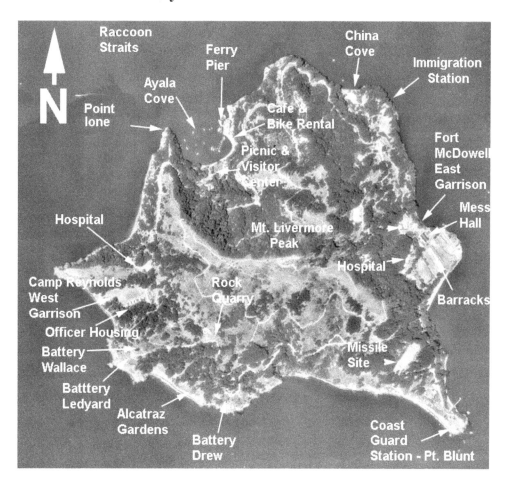

A blueprint of the island

About Charles River Editors

Charles River Editors is a boutique digital publishing company, specializing in bringing history back to life with educational and engaging books on a wide range of topics. Keep up to date with our new and free offerings with this 5 second sign up on our weekly mailing list, and visit Our Kindle Author Page to see other recently published Kindle titles.

We make these books for you and always want to know our readers' opinions, so we encourage you to leave reviews and look forward to publishing new and exciting titles each week.

Introduction

A picture of Angel Island from the Angel Island Ferry

Angel Island

"The boat was launched and I set out to search for better anchorage for the ship. I went out toward the island I named de los Angeles [Angel Island], which is the largest in this harbor, in search of proper moorings for making water and wood; and though I found some good ones, I rather preferred to pass onward in search of another island, which when I reached it proved so arid and steep there was not even a boat-harbor there; I named this island La Isla de los Alcatraces [Island of the Pelicans] because of their being so plentiful there." - Juan Manuel de Ayala, 1775

Juan Manuel de Ayala

Angel Island, the largest island in San Francisco Bay at about 740 acres, was originally named when Don Juan Manuel Ayala sailed into San Francisco Bay. Supposedly, the island was named "Angel" because the land mass appeared to him as an angel guarding the bay, and when Ayala made a map of the Bay, on it he marked Angel Island as, "Isla de Los Angeles."[1] This would remain the island's name ever since, even as the use of the island would certainly change over time.

The island is currently a large state park with beautiful views of the San Francisco Bay and skyline, but the most noteworthy part of the park is the immigration museum. That site is what makes Angel Island so famous today, as it remains best known for being the entry point for Asian immigrants to the United States from 1910-1940.[2] There is no way to know for sure how many people actually passed through Angel Island because of the destruction of most of the historical documentation in a fire, but historians estimate that it was between 100,000 and 500,000 people.

For the first century of American history, there were no restrictions on immigration, and this

---

[1] Flanagan, Alice K. *Angel Island*. Minneapolis, MN: Compass Point Books, 2006. 10
[2] Journal of American ethnic history 3

open immigration policy was something the Founding Fathers desired for a young, small country. In 1790, Congress passed a law allowing people to become naturalized citizens if they resided in America for two years and stayed in the same state for a year.

In the late 19th century, however, growing support for the eugenics movement drove the United States to develop harsher immigration laws. These laws were solely to ensure that other races from "undesirable" countries did not contaminate the ethnic "purity" within the United States. In the 1870s, The Chinese Exclusion Act was passed, and it restricted Chinese immigrants from become naturalized citizens. Additionally, laborers were unable to come to the United States, and those who immigrated had to already have relatives in the country. These discriminatory policies came in response to the huge number of Chinese workers who headed for the West Coast to work on the Transcontinental Railroad. In 1884, this law was reinforced, and immigrants who were previously allowed to come and go as they please had issues reentering the country if they left. The Geary Act added even more restrictions on Chinese immigrants in 1892.

Japan and the United States also reached a number of agreements that affected immigration policy. The Gentlemen's Agreement in 1907 had the Japanese government stop approving passports to citizens, and an 1882 law also prohibited people with mental health issues and physical diseases from entering the country. In 1917, the biggest piece of legislature thus far on immigration was passed. It is often referred to as the Asiatic Barred Zone Act, due to how largely it affected Asian immigrants. This law created more justifications for excluding immigrants, including illiteracy. This was the first time a quota system was introduced, and it led to a noticeable decrease in immigration to the United States.

In 1921, the Emergency Quota Act was passed, and it took things even further against Asian immigrants, this time preventing immigration from Asia completely. It set the immigrant quota from countries outside of the Western hemisphere to 165,000. The Chinese Exclusion laws were appealed in 1943, and in 1965, The Immigration and Nationality Amendments were passed, which put an end to ethnic based quota systems.

Angel Island is often referred to the Ellis Island of the West, but many argue that they are extremely different in their preservation of immigrant histories. For one, Angel Island took much longer to preserve, and the preservation of Ellis Island focuses on the positive reception of European immigrants on the East Coast, which plays well to corporate sponsors and the American story. Historian John Bodnar explained that Ellis Island represents "the view of American history as a steady succession progress and uplift for ordinary people."[3] Ellis Island fits nicely into the narrative of the American Dream, because even though the immigrants who came through there were subject to racism, they were predominantly white. Angel Island was a much more multiracial experience, and when recounting its history, the tensions of exclusiveness

[3] Lee, Erika, and Judy Yung. *Angel Island: Immigrant Gateway to America*. New York: Oxford Univ. Press, 2012.

and xenophobia that existed in the late 19th century and early 20th century are laid bare for all to see.

After a fire in 1940, Angel Island went from being an immigration station to being used for military purposes. At first, it was used as POW holding facility during World War II, and then finally as a Nike missile base between 1954 and 1962. After a long fight to preserve the island's history as an immigration station and a huge pillar of Asian-American history, the island was declared a landmark in 1996, and the museum opened with a fully restored immigration station in 2009. Today, the island can be visited by the public via a ferry from San Francisco, and countless people hike and bike the island, as well as taking tours of the immigration station.

Angel Island: The History and Legacy of the Immigration Center in San Francisco Bay examines the frequently overlooked station, and what the experience was like there for immigrants. Along with pictures depicting important people, places, and events, you will learn about Angel Island like never before.

Angel Island's Other Uses

While it is most famous as an immigration station, prior to 1910 there were many uses for Angel Island. Evidence of Miwok natives has been found on the island dating back an estimated 3,000 years, but when Europeans began to use the island while going through the Golden Gate, it devastated the Miwok population previously living there.

Before it was ever officially a part of the United States, many ethnic groups from different countries used Angel Island for different reasons. Russian sealers used it to store their furs, and whalers used it in order to find supplies such as water and firewood. It was also used by smugglers in order to escape customs officials, a common occurrence when it was under Spanish control. Smugglers continued to use it to avoid United States customs officers.[4]

[4] Daniels, Roger. "No Lamps Were Lit for Them." *No Lamps Were Lit for Them: Angel Island and the Historiography of Asian American Immigration* 17, no. 1, 3-18. Accessed May 29, 2019. https://www.jstor.org/stable/27502236. 4

Kai Schreiber's picture of Alcatraz and San Francisco from Angel Island

A picture of Angel Island's port

The island was largely ignored until the mid-19th century, when the United States government built a fort there. In his memoirs, a famous general wrote of his time spent at the Presidio in San Francisco in the late 1840s, after the region had just recently come under American control. 15 years before his occupation of Atlanta and "March to the Sea" made William Tecumseh Sherman the scourge of the South, Sherman noted how steep the bluffs were and the natural geography of the surrounding area. The area's main fort, the Presidio, was not in good shape when the United States took possession of the fort and the small surrounding settlement from Mexico in 1847. The Americans changed the name of the settlement from Yerba Buena to San Francisco, and the country immediately set about strengthening the area's defenses across the Bay. Right next to the Golden Gate Bridge is Fort Point, constructed just before the Civil War broke out, and over the next 100 years, dozens of batteries were installed, a coast guard station was added, and barracks with parade grounds were built to man the Presidio.

The remains of an artillery battery on Angel Island

Camp Reynolds was built on the island in 1842 by American soldiers, and Angel Island would be used as a military station off and on until. The military constructed Fort McDowell during the Civil War to deal with Confederate sympathizers who were in the Bay Area. The installations on the island were also used to counter the Apache, the Sioux, and the Modoc tribes.[5]

[5]California State Parks, State Of California. "US Army on the Island." CA State Parks. Accessed May 24, 2019.
https://www.parks.ca.gov/?page_id=1307.

A picture of the remains of Camp Reynolds

The infrastructure for the immigration station began to be built when Angel Island was used as a military base. There were barracks and hospitals on the island, and in 1891, thanks to the threat of the Bubonic plague, Angel Island was used as a quarantine station in order to screen passengers arriving to the island from other countries. Originally, when the plague was suspected in San Francisco's Chinatown, they quarantined local areas on Angel Island to ensure that the plague would not spread.

The quarantine station would form the basis for the island's transformation into an immigration station, and in the early 20th century, construction would begin on the island to make it a functional immigration station. The quarantine station was converted and outfitted with disinfection facilities, barracks, and hospitals, allowing Angel Island to function as an immigration center until 1940, after which it served as a POW camp, a missile base, and a state park.

Anything but Angelic

While Angel Island was originally built to be for all immigrants, and a large influx of European immigrants was expected, the start of American involvement in World War I in 1917 made it less possible for Europeans to immigrate to the United States via the West Coast. As a result, a vast majority of immigrants who came through Angel Island were of Asian descent – about 33% of the immigrants processed on Angel Island were from China, another 33% came from Japan, and the remaining 33% came from places such as Russia, Europe, Mexico, the Americas, New Zealand, and Australia.

To this day, Angel Island remains notorious for the mistreatment of immigrants who were processed in the immigration station. The conditions for many "undesirable" ethnic groups who arrived there were deplorable, and ethnicity essentially determined an individual's treatment on Angel Island. Angel Island is often referred to as the Ellis Island of the West, but there are some key differences between the door, starting with the different ethnic groups each coast accepted on their immigration stations.

Once immigrants arrived on Angel Island, they were separated based on gender, age, and ethnicity, which determined whether parents and their children stayed together. Once they arrived and were separated, they were then taken to the doctor at a hospital site on the island, where immigrants were always checked for diseases. In 1910, officials examined over 11,000 immigrants, and in 1920, 25,000 people were examined.[6] There were many diseases that doctors were on the lookout for, and exclusion could happen if any patients were found to have heart disease, tuberculosis, syphilis, gonorrhea, or leprosy. On a case-to-case basis, this could also happen if the individual had a hernia, pregnancy, "poor physique," or "nervous affectations"[7] Thus, it was easy for an immigrant to be deported on the whims of one of the doctors in the hospital, and in general, inspectors tried to weed out those would be unable to work when they entered the United States. Even the eyes of patients were scanned in order to check for trachoma, a bacterial infection of the eye which one can detect on the surface of the eyelids. If a patient was believed to have trachoma, they would be deemed unfit to work in the United States and unable to support themselves.

Many accounts of immigrants indicate they detested the lack of humanity that occurred during their examinations. They were treated as though they were already criminals or diseased patients, and often they were experimented on. There was also a lack of sanitation overall on the island, which was especially noticeable in the hospital. There was no hot water, no toilets, and poor ventilation.[8] Some of this was due to institutionalized racism - many government officials who were responsible for the immigration station believed that the health conditions on the island were fit for the Asian immigrants who made up the majority of the population on the island. Public officials were aware of the lack of sanitary conditions, and at one point this would kill three patients who were infected with spinal meningitis after one of the rooms was not properly disinfected.[9]

---

[6] Ibid 24
[7] Ibid 36
[8] Lee, Erika, and Judy Yung. *Angel Island: Immigrant Gateway to America*. New York: Oxford Univ. Press, 2012.38.
[9] Ibid, 28

While immigrants who came to Ellis Island in New York City were also subject to medical examinations, the ones on Angel Island are known to have been more invasive. Racist inspectors simply believed that those entering from Asian countries were automatically diseased. South Asian and Chinese passengers were subject to the most scrutiny, as they were suspected of carrying more diseases and parasites that could harm the general American population.

There were a number of employees who worked on the island at the immigration station, including mantanaince people, inspectors, stenographers, deckhands, engineers, and telephone operators. There also were plumbers, cooks, and laundrymen who kept the island fucntioning on a daily basis. In the 1920s, there were 137 employees working on Angel Island, and some of these individuals even lived on the island. The cooks and those who worked in the hospital lived there year round in cottages on the island, and some of the employees lived on the island with their families. In fact, many of the jobs on Angel Island were coveted, as they were considered good positions to have to advance a career in politics.

Those who sought out jobs on the island would soon face moral challenges. Many of them were overwhelmed by the amount of work, which could not be properly handled by one person. Examples of this can be found in the diary entries of Inspector John Birge Sawyer, which also outlined the incredibly ineffective ways in which the Chinese Exclusion Act laws played out on the island.

While Sawyer's account demonstrated the regret he felt over being unable to more effectively carry out the country's immigration laws, not all officers were like him. Commissioner of Immigration Samuel W. Backus admitted at a conference in 1915 that he was, "opposed to Oriental immigration" from "all standpoints."[10] There was such a big gap in the opinions towards immigrants among those who were working there that it was hard for the staff to maintain any sort of consistency when it came to enforcing politces, especially towards Chinese immigrants. The staff that was hired on the island was mostly male. Some women were hired, but none of them were ever appointed as immigrant inspectors.

---

[10] Lee, Erika, and Judy Yung. *Angel Island: Immigrant Gateway to America*. New York: Oxford Univ. Press, 2012.

42

Backus

When the Chinese Exclusion Act started to go into effect, hiring Chinese employees was prohibited, as the government did not believe they could be trustworthy when it came to jobs on Angel Island. As a result, there were often mistranslations that occurred between Chinese immigrants and inspectors, and this prohibition remained in effect until 1914, when it became abundantly clear that it was too impractical to not have those fluent in Chinese, Japanese, and other Asian languages working at the immigration station.[11] This would make inspections much smoother and clearer for everyone involved.

Regardless of who worked there, racism continued to be extremely prevalent on Angel Island. Some accounts note that whites who came from Australia and New Zealand received preferential treatment, and this was all but formalized in 1921, when government legislation ensured all immigrants from Australia and New Zealand could potentially be let into the United States regardless of the quota laws that had just gone into effect.[12] A letter from Ivy Gidlow, a Canadian immigrant residing on Angel Island, described "clean white rooms," "colorful people [in] the dining halls," and the "comfort" of the immigration station. Gidlow had access to hot baths and a well-stocked library. Gidlow wrote, "I am almost content here"[13]

---

[11] I Lee, Erika, and Judy Yung. *Angel Island: Immigrant Gateway to America*. New York: Oxford Univ. Press, 2012. 52.

[12] Lee, Erika, and Judy Yung. *Angel Island: Immigrant Gateway to America*. New York: Oxford Univ. Press, 2012.

5

There was also an issue of racism among immigration lawyers, which obviously was a huge issue for the immigrants they represented. One famous immigration attorney, Joseph P. Fallon, asserted that European immigrants should be allowed in because they continued to make the country a great place: "It is the purpose of the American people to increase the efficiency of the race by encouraging, stimulating, and increasing European immigration to our shores; the Finn, the Bohemian, the Italian, the Greek, the Spaniard, the Russian, the Pole, the Israelite, the Magyar, we need them all."[14] This was all the more disturbing given that he was representing a large number of Asian clients, especially Chinese immigrants.

Class also came into play on Angel Island, as those immigrants who came from wealthy economic backgrounds had an easier time getting into the country. Those who traveled in first class on the boats they came on were given preferential treatment.[15] While some might have looked down on Mexican or Chinese immigrants based on race, if people from these same countries had wealth, it helped them in the process. If immigrants were members of laboring classes, they were quickly discriminated against, especially if they were Chinese. Immigrants were constantly judged on their appearance and their skill sets.

Arrivals were also treated differently based on their gender. If a woman was Chinese or Japanese, they were only allowed into the country if they could prove that they were dependent on their husband or father. Most women were not admitted independently, and those who were working class were very much unwanted. Women who were traveling alone were often thought of as suspicious, since according to officials they likely had a troubled moral past if they were traveling alone.[16] If was also assumed that if they were travelling alone, they would not be able to support themselves and were thus a liability for the country. One woman wrote, "I was forced to come to America and marry a man I had never seen before. The Japanese were bombing us and there was nowhere else to go. My mother wanted me to come to America so that I could bring the family over later. Whenever we saw anyone laving, we would cry, especially those of us who had been there a long time...I must have cried a bowlful during my stay at Angel Island."[17]

Meal times were often over crowded, and nutrition was never a priority. There were two different mess halls for eating meals. One had wooden tables and was for Asian men, while the other dining room was called the oil cloth dining room because it was used by Europeans and Asian women. These separation of men and women were used to alienate and reinforce racial stereotypes of the time. The two dining rooms also had two different types of food; the Asian male dining room was served with less food, and the food was prepared by Chinese-American cooks.

---

[13] Ibid. 5
[14] Ibid. 51
[15] Ibid. 51
[16] Lee, Erika, and Judy Yung. *Angel Island: Immigrant Gateway to America.* New York: Oxford Univ. Press, 2012. 52
[17] Ibid article 55

It is hard to look at the glaring differences between immigrants coming to Angel Island without looking at how much institutionalized governmental racism played into the immigrants' experiences. Asian immigrants who arrived at the island were at the mercy of the racist government officials and would often be deported immediately. Moreover, after arriving in the San Francisco Wharf via boat, Asian immigrants were immediately taken to Angel Island on another boat, often after weeks of sea sickness. They would be told to leave all of their luggage and then go to the barracks, where they were subjected to humiliating medical examinations. One account recalled, "About ten of us were taken to a big room and ordered to strip naked for an examination. We were told to give samples of urines and feces. Since we had not been warned ahead of time, some of us couldn't. The examination took about one hour and was cursory. We felt extremely embarrassed, not being accustomed to appearing naked in public."[18]

Naturally, many immigrants resented the fact that they were caged like animals on Angel Island. They did not like being apart from their families, and at the same time, their own discriminatory attitudes made intermingling with each other difficult. Some upper class women hated having to stay in the same living quarters as women who were unmarried or considered to have immoral pasts.

Chinese Immigrants' Experiences

Angel Island wasn't an enjoyable experience for most, but Chinese immigrants, who represented the biggest portion of arrivals, were subjected to the most racist policies thanks to the Chinese Exclusion Act of 1882 and thus had to endure many inhumane conditions. Chinese immigrants who stayed on Angel Island were often kept there the longest, and they are mostly responsible for the poetry preserved on the walls of the living quarters.

Immigrants from China to the United States already had a long, complicated history, starting in the 1840s. The first flow of Chinese immigrants to the West Coast had started in earnest after a crop failure in southern China that caused the custom houses in San Francisco to swell with 20,026 Chinese arrivals. Even more Chinese came as news reached China about the apparent ease of mining in California. By the end of the 1940s, nearly 20% of the population of the Southern Mines consisted of Chinese miners, and they would become known as the most industrious and tireless of the miners, finding gold in claims that previous owners had thought depleted and persisting in mining an area far longer than others who eventually left the fields altogether.

However, other miners reacted to their presence negatively, and in some cases Chinese miners had their camps violently attacked. The state government attempted to rectify the problem through the creation of a second Miner's Tax, but unfortunately this only seemed to accelerate

---

[18] Yung, Judy. "A Bowlful of Tears: Chinese Women Immigrants." *Frontiers: A Journal of Women Studies* 2, no. 2, 52-55. Accessed May 19, 2019. https://www.jstor.org/stable/3346011.2.

other miners' attacks on Chinese camps. Reports in the same year indicated that an epidemic of robberies hit the immigrant miners from China, close to 200 alone, along with a series of murders.

All of this partly explains why the Chinese decided to diversify and choose occupations that did not put them into open competition with white American miners. Another reason, and one closer to the financial windfalls that occurred during the Gold Rush, is explained by the chance for profit in the mercantile and service industries. The Chinese moved into the laundry business, other domestic services, and later railroad building, all of which necessarily thrived as the population in the region boomed.

Word soon reached the Kwangtung province that America was hiring many men to build its new railroad, and after years of famine, many Chinese families needed a new start. Thus, Chinese men began flooding into California to seek fortunes not in gold but in shiny iron rails, and by 1866, 80% of the West Coast railroad workforce was made up of Chinese immigrants. In 1867, author Albert Richardson wrote, "The cars now run nearly to the summit of the Sierras. At the time of my visit the terminus was Colfax, fifty-five miles east of Sacramento. Thence we took horses for twelve miles. Upon this little section of road four thousand laborers were at work—one-tenth Irish, the rest Chinese. They were a great army laying siege to Nature in her strongest citadel. The rugged mountains looked like stupendous ant-hills. They swarmed with Celestials, shoveling, wheeling, carting, drilling and blasting rocks and earth, while their dull, moony eyes stared out from under immense basket-hats, like umbrellas. At several dining camps we saw hundreds sitting on the ground, eating soft boiled rice with chopsticks as fast as terrestrials could with soup-ladles. Irish laborers received thirty dollars per month (gold) and board; Chinese, thirty-one dollars, boarding themselves. After a little experience the latter were quite as efficient and far less troublesome. The Hudson Bay Company in its balmy days was compelled to import laborers from the Sandwich Islands; and without the Chinese the California end of the great national thoroughfare must have been delayed for many years. Twelve thousand are now employed upon it."

David Haward Bain, author of *Empire Express: Building the First Transcontinental Railroad*, described the situation: "The peasants of Kwangtung were indentured in California to locally run Chinese district companies, signed on for up to five years of labor at comparatively low wages until their tickets were paid; they then filtered out into the streams and rivers of the Sierra slope in search of gold. Enforcement thugs and old-world penalties awaited slackers and deserters, but the life, hard as it was, promised rewards, particularly the hope that two or three hundred dollars could be amassed— enough by Kwangtung standards for a return home and a luxury retirement. Until that happy time, which rarely attended any of the immigrants, there were only the diversions of gambling, prostitution, and opium, establishments for which sprang up in the Chinatowns of San Francisco, Sacramento, Stockton, and Marysville, and in the smaller mountainside encampments beneath roofs of canvas."

A picture of Chinese workers on the Transcontinental Railroad

Through it all, Americans were not thrilled with the mass influx of Chinese immigrants in the mid-19th century. While they were treated as cheap and easy labor, Chinese immigrants were viewed as foreign and bad for the economy. Many Californians were replaced with Chinese labor, and whites directly blamed the immigrants instead of the government or the companies that hired them. As a result of mass protests, many Californians demanded that Congress pass immigration laws restricting the Chinese, and in 1882, Congress responded by passing the Chinese Exclusion Act, which refused entry to many Chinese immigrants. The only people exempted from the law were high-ranking officials, students, tourists, the wives of Americans who happened to be Chinese. After this law was passed, it became so difficult to enter the United States for Chinese people that many often lied about their background or claimed that they were the children of American parents.

The opening of Angel Island as an immigration station is often considered a direct response to anti-Chinese legislature. The Chinese Exclusion Act made it impossible to hire Chinese laborers, which really affected the Chinese population in the United States. Moreover, the act was made permanent during Theodore Roosevelt's presidency. [19] Before the opening of the immigration

[19] Daniels, Roger. "No Lamps Were Lit for Them." *No Lamps Were Lit for Them: Angel Island and the Historiography of Asian American Immigration* 17, no. 1, 3-18. Accessed May 29, 2019.

center on Angel Island, Chinese immigrants were taken to a warehouse in the Pacific Mail Steamship Company upon their arrival, and it was an extremely overcrowded space with up to 200 people in it at a time.

In the late 19th century, there was a push by the government to develop a better solution to deal with Chinese immigrants. In 1904, Congress had Secretary of Commerce and Labor Walter Metcalf investigate the plan for an immigrant station on Angel Island. Metcalf and an Oakland architect named Walter J. Mathews drew up a plan that would cost $250,000. [20] The island's north shore was referred to as China Cove, and it became a big complex with a lot of different buildings. These buildings included an administration building, a wharf, a hospital, and a detention barracks.

Mathews based his designs for the Angel Island immigration station on Ellis Island, although there were some obvious differences. For one, Angel Island's buildings were constructed out of wood, whereas Ellis Island's buildings were made out of brick.[21] Some of this likely had to do with the different weather conditions on the two coasts, and many of the wooden buildings would be destroyed when they caught fire in 1940, taking many administrative records with them.

Even when the buildings were brand new and officially opened, there were many staff members who were unhappy about the conditions. A 1909 report on the buildings showed a long list of issues, including a lack of fire protection and a limited water supply.[22] One building administrator complained that the buildings were "dangerous firetraps, unsanitary, and vermin infested."[23] This was in 1910, when the building was first opened, so one can only imagine what the buildings looked like after several decades. The hospital was not properly outfitted, and the kitchen was noted to be infested with cockroaches by the Public Health Services Surgeon. Additionally, each room, which was built to hold a maximum of 10 people, often had 54 beds in it, complete with people for each one of them.[24]

Traveling the Pacific to the United States often took as long as two months, which was obviously taxing on immigrants.[25] Those who were poor were forced to travel in steerage, where many were affected by illness and some died before arriving. The conditions ensured that by the time they reached Angel Island, Chinese immigrants were often under an immense amount of

---

https://www.jstor.org/stable/27502236. 4.
[20] Ibid.
[21] Ibid
[22] Lee, Erika, and Judy Yung. *Angel Island: Immigrant Gateway to America.* New York: Oxford Univ. Press, 2012. 2
[23] Daniels, Roger. "No Lamps Were Lit for Them." *No Lamps Were Lit for Them: Angel Island and the Historiography of Asian American Immigration* 17, no. 1, 3-18. Accessed May 29, 2019. https://www.jstor.org/stable/27502236
[24] Ibid. 5
[25] Flanagan, Alice K. *Angel Island.* Minneapolis, MN: Compass Point Books, 2006. 15

physical and mental stress.

In fact, some would commit suicide on the island. In 1919, Fong Food, who was on his way from China to Mexico, tied himself to a gas fixture with a towel and hung himself after a few days in the detention center. Other suicides in the men's barracks occurred in 1931 and 1936. One man used a necktie in order to hang himself, and one woman reportedly stabbed herself through the brain with a chopstick.

Soto Shee attempted suicide on the island after the death of her seven-month-old son, Soon Din, in 1924. Soon Din died due to gastroenteritis, and his body was taken to San Francisco for burial, where his mother was not allowed to go due to her detainment. She was so distraught that she tried to hang herself in the bathroom. She was quickly found by another woman and taken to the hospital, but even her suicide attempt did not persuade immigration officials that she was under mental stress and needed to be admitted into the country. In time, some women accompanied others to the bathroom to prevent them from attempting suicide.[26]

As the suicide attempts suggest, the Chinese immigrants who arrived on the island were often subject to a long line of questioning, and even those who claimed American citizenship would have to answers hours of questioning. One Chinese immigrant was detained for two years.[27]

The line of questioning was invasive, and it was a lengthy process clearly intended to catch any mistakes in order to deport people as quickly as possible. Chinese immigrants were asked about several generations of their supposed family, as far as three generations back. They needed to know the layout of their villages and family homes, even down to the number of steps in the house. They were expected to know the "burial sites of their grandparents, the directions in which their family houses faced, the number of houses in the village and their arrangement, the names of the neighbors, and even a description of the village market."[28] All of this was a lot of information for them to memorize, which is why study books were often given out to help during travel.

There was an expected line of questioning, but occasionally one of the inspectors would ask something unexpected. If they did so, the Chinese staff in the kitchen was used to translate. These same cooks also hid messages from other family members of those on the island in the food.

[26] Lee, Erika, and Judy Yung. *Angel Island: Immigrant Gateway to America*. New York: Oxford Univ. Press, 2012. 109.

[27] Daniels, Roger. "No Lamps Were Lit for Them." *No Lamps Were Lit for Them: Angel Island and the Historiography of Asian American Immigration* 17, no. 1, 3-18. Accessed May 29, 2019. https://www.jstor.org/stable/27502236. 8.

[28] Yung, Judy. "A Bowlful of Tears: Chinese Women Immigrants." *Frontiers: A Journal of Women Studies* 2, no. 2, 52-55. Accessed May 19, 2019. https://www.jstor.org/stable/3346011. 54.

There were certainly cases of recorded bribery, and this would often help people get through immigration hearings. In 1917, a graft ring was discovered on the island, and several immigration officers were convicted. The ones involved in this ring were transferred to other posts or fired, and this led to the end of some of the intense bribery that had been occurring.[29] Some corrupt immigration officials would also pass along coaching information for a small fee. If one failed the questioning and was deported back to China, he or she would be excluded from entering the United States, sent immediately back, and had no right to appeal the decision to the courts.

It was easy for Chinese women to get labled as having a questionable moral past by immigration inspectors who would do anything to make them feel uncomfortable at their hearings. A lot of these "questionable pasts" had to do with sex, which women were interviewed about explicitly in their immigration hearings.[30] Keeping in mind that there were no female immigation inspectors, it was all the more embarassing for women to go through these hearings. Some women who arrived unmarried were the subject of intense questioning, as evidenced by the documented interview of an unmarried Swedish woman who arrived on Angel Island. Her interviewer asked her, "Were you a virtuous woman when you first arrived to the US from Sweden?" He also asked her, "Who was the cause of of you losing your virtue in Sweden?"[31] The woman involved in this line of questioning, Maria Holmgren was ultimately denied entry as "a person admitting a misdemeanor involving moral turptitude..having had immoral relations with men prior to [her] arrival in the United States"[32] Questions were even more invasive if the immigrant was a woman of color.

Likewise, the medical examinations that occurred on the island were extremely difficult for Chinese immigrants. Culturally, they were not used to undressing in public and were often humiliated when asked to strip down in front of white hospital inspectors. In one interview, Mr. Lee, a Chinese immigrant who came to the United States in 1930, recalled, "When we first came, we went to the hospital building for the physical examination. The doctor told us to take off everything. Really though, it was the Chinese never expose themselves like that. They checked you and checked you. We never got used to that kind of thing—and in front of whites."[33] One woman who was subjected to the medical examinations asked, "Was it really a physical exam or was it designed to insult our entire race?" [34]

---

[29] Ibid. 55.

[30] Lee, Erika, and Judy Yung. *Angel Island: Immigrant Gateway to America*. New York: Oxford Univ. Press, 2012. 52

53.

[31]Lee, Erika, and Judy Yung. *Angel Island: Immigrant Gateway to America*. New York: Oxford Univ. Press, 2012. 54

[32] Ibid. 54

[33] Lee, Erika, and Judy Yung. *Angel Island: Immigrant Gateway to America*. New York: Oxford Univ. Press, 2012. 76.

[34] Ibid. 77.

After the medical examination, Chinese immigrants would be detained and essentially imprisoned on Angel Island for long periods of time. There were four categories of Chinese immigrants allowed on the island: diplomats, merchants, families, and people who could already claim American citizenship. No laborers or their families were allowed into the country after The Chinese Exclusion Act. The law was eventually repealed in 1943, but prior to that it was extremely difficult to get Chinese immigrants into the United States.

Once the laws were passed, many Chinese immigrants tried to go through the court system to gain entry into the United States. Many people sued under the 14th Amendment of the United States. Bribery was a tactic used. One woman claimed she was only released after three days because she was able to give $600 to the people in charge of the immigration process. The same woman reported that she was treated better once it was known that she had money to spread around, and that her family could take their luggage from the luggage holding facility while everyone else had to leave theirs. When it was time for her to leave, she was helped, and in general the staff was nicer to her.[35]

Some Chinese immigrants would have wind up staying on the island for questioning for 6 months to a year or more, and though they weren't considered guilty of anything, they were still locked in the barracks on the island. Men and women were separated, which meant a lot of people were denied access to their partners. They were only allowed to go to the storage units that their personal belongings were stored in one designated time a week. There were two or three bunk beds stacked on top of one another, making it hardly the most comfortable of living quarters. There were a lot more Chinese men than women, so it was a little bit roomier for the women in their living areas - some accounts state that there would be no more than 30 women in the female living quarters, but there could be anywhere from 40-100 men. Some young boys could stay with their mothers, but any of them that were over the age of 10 were required to go to the adult male barracks. Nobody was allowed visitors for fears they would be coached on how to act during interrogations.

Some missionaries visited the island. Katharine Maurer, the "Angel of Angel Island," often came in as a missionary and provided outside information and needlework for the women. [36] Maurer's official title was deaconess at the Angel Island Immigration Station, but on the island she hosted religious teaching, English classes, and offered her general friendship. [37] There was very little that the immigrants, who lived like prisoners, could do. Some of them knit or did needlework, and they were occasionally allowed to go on a walk. There are some accounts of them being given dominos to play with, but most of them "sat on beds behind locked doors." [38]

[35] Yung, Judy. "A Bowlful of Tears: Chinese Women Immigrants." *Frontiers: A Journal of Women Studies* 2, no. 2, 52-55. Accessed May 19, 2019. https://www.jstor.org/stable/3346011.2. 53
[36] Lee, Erika, and Judy Yung. *Angel Island: Immigrant Gateway to America*. New York: Oxford Univ. Press, 2012. 53
[37] Ibid.

Language barriers also posed problems for Chinese immigrants on the island, even amongst each other. While all immigrants from China were housed in the same sector, not all of them spoke the same dialects.

The meals that they ate often did not include enough food, and the meals were prepared by Chinese cooks who admitted they would not personally eat the food. One woman staying on Angel Island recounted, "The squash were all chopped and thrown together like pig slop. The pork was in big, big chunks. Everything thrown into a big bowl that resembled a wash tub, left there for you to eat or not. They just steamed the food till it was like a soupy stew. After looking at it, you'd lose your appetite." [39]

When one of the cooks was interviewed, he explained that the meals included soup, rice, salted fish, dried pork, potatoes dried greens, and sand dabs. The same cook also stated that there was a huge riot over the food in 1923. Dishes were thrown around the dining room, and eventually the Chinese Consul General came and explained that the menu was fixed by government agreement. Soldiers then forced the rioters into their quarters, and some immigrants refused to eat the food for three days. Even though this occurred, the cook recalled that no changes to the food were made.

Some people did have relatives send food from San Francisco, so occasionally those on Angel Island had access to roast duck, barbecued pork, and sausages.[40] Additionally, if detainees had any money, it was possible for them to buy other kinds of food in the back of the dining room, such as canned fish, bean cakes, fresh fruit, ice cream, and peanuts. Gerald Won explained, "We would put a little money on the table and the cook would give us the best they had."[41] showing that bribery of the cooks was also a way to stay well fed.

The separation at mealtimes between men and women also ensured that there was a clear separation between Chinese men and women at almost all times on the island. This often separated families, and it also meant men and women had to form their own social groups. The Chinese women were not as organized as the men , who often had access to the organization Zizhihui, also known as the Angel Island Libery Association, which was formed in 1922.[42] This organization was formed by detainees and helped them keep some sense of order within their community. It was a little easier for newer immigrants arriving to the island to adjust with the

[38] Yung, Judy. "A Bowlful of Tears: Chinese Women Immigrants." *Frontiers: A Journal of Women Studies* 2, no. 2, 52-55. Accessed May 19, 2019. https://www.jstor.org/stable/3346011.53.

[38] Ibid.

[39] Yung, Judy. "A Bowlful of Tears: Chinese Women Immigrants." *Frontiers: A Journal of Women Studies* 2, no. 2, 52-55. Accessed May 19, 2019. https://www.jstor.org/stable/3346011.54

[40] Ibid. 54

[41] Lee, Erika, and Judy Yung. *Angel Island: Immigrant Gateway to America*. New York: Oxford Univ. Press, 2012. 98

[42] Ibid. 98

Liberty Association - when they arrived, there was someone who would share with them the ins and outs of the island, as well as what the rules were. This group had membership dues, which were used to buy books, school supplies, and recreational equiment. There were scheduled events through this group, and an arbitration committee that went between immigrants and inspectors. At one point, this group negotiated more toilet paper and soap for detainees, and a school for the children on the island. [43]

Conversely, the women did not have the advantage of assembling a community or groups. There was very little for them to do, and many of them lacked the formal education to read materials sent over to them from San Francisco. While there was no formal group bonding them together, many women still formed close relationships to help them deal with the entire process. One woman observed that many Japanese people would leave Angel Island within 24 hours, while they were forced into long periods of confinement.[44]

Given the exclusionary policies against Chinese immigrants, many of them who came to Angel Island were suspected of being "paper immigrants," the term for fake sons and daughters that some Chinese people who had previously immigrated reported they had back in China. In 1906, the Hall of Records was destroyed in San Francisco, which helped many immigrants commit fraud. Many Chinese residents claimed citizenship and added their own family to the new paperwork. It was possible to buy a spot in someone's family on their paperwork when it was redone, comprising one of the forms of pushback Chinese immigrants used against the government. With no way to prove whether they were previously residents, it was relatively easier to forge documents and get immigrants in.[45]

One of the ways in which Chinese immigrants were able to do this is that when someone who had successfully immigrated went back to China, they would report the birth of a son. This allowed some leeway with documents once other immigrants arrived in the United States. It was so hard to prove who was a citizen after the fire that in the 1920s and 1930s, more Chinese people entered the United States with the citizenship loophole than any other ethnic group.[46]

In order to get their paperwork to be admitted into San Francisco, the detainees had to go through a lot of questioning. Many of them studied coaching materials, as there was a specific way in which they should answer questions. These books were studied before coming to America, often on the boat, and they were illegal, so immigrants often had to tear them up when on the boat. Inspectors were obsessed with determining whether immigrants could answer

---

[43] Lee, Erika, and Judy Yung. *Angel Island: Immigrant Gateway to America*. New York: Oxford Univ. Press, 2012. 99

[44] Ibid. 98.

[45] Daniels, Roger. "No Lamps Were Lit for Them." *No Lamps Were Lit for Them: Angel Island and the Historiography of Asian American Immigration* 17, no. 1, 3-18. Accessed May 29, 2019. https://www.jstor.org/stable/27502236.

[46] Lee, Erika, and Judy Yung. *Angel Island: Immigrant Gateway to America*. New York: Oxford Univ. Press, 2012.

questions and prove that they were a part of the family they claimed.

Immigration officials in the United States believed that following the fire of 1906, 90% of Chinese citizenship claims were fake. Whether that estimate was close to accurate, there's no doubt that immigration fraud was rampant, with Chinese companies often partnering up with Chinese people born in the United States. As a result, even families who had previously been in the United States legally had issues when they were being questioned on Angel Island. Some inspectors used intimidation and aggression in order to test Chinese applicants, and while eventually immigration officials figured it out, there was an interesting tactic that Chinese immigrants used at one point with fake American coins. The coins were made to look like nickels and quarters, but on the back there were answers to an immigration interrogation in Chinese characters. There was also an incident of peanuts being pried apart and glued back together with messages inside on how to pass the interrogation. [47]

These interrogations were so intense that there were reports of real family members failing them. One man reported that he failed because he said the floor under his bed was brick, while his father had answered that it was dirt. He claimed, "It was a dirt floor and then changed to brick when my father left for America."[48] This is one of the reasons why he failed his interrogation, even though he was not a paper son.

Chinese immigrants dealt with racism on all fronts, including from other immigrants. An example of this kind of internal Angel Island racism can be seen in one case when German crew members from a merchant vessel were housed in the same place as Chinese immigrants and demanded they be given a separate room. In writing, they asserted that "some relief must be given us that we do not have to live in the company of Chinamen, with whom we are obliged to take even our meals in the same room. This destroys our appetite, which is not improved by the monotonous fare."[49]

Morale was often low for Chinese immigrants, which was reflected in the poems. One detainee wrote, "I clasped my hands in parting with my brothers and classmates. Because of the mouth, I hastened to cross the American Ocean. How was I to know that the western barbarians had lost their hearts and reason? With a hundred kinds of oppressive laws, they mistreat us Chinese."[50]

The poems on Angel Island were first noticed by a park ranger named Alexander Weiss, just as Angel Island was being slated for destruction. Fearing the poems would be lost, in 1972 Weiss contacted Dr. George Araki of San Francisco State University. He and his partner, Mak

---

[47] Ibid, 90

[48] Ibid

[49] Lee, Erika, and Judy Yung. *Angel Island: Immigrant Gateway to America*. New York: Oxford Univ. Press, 2012. 58

[50] Lee, Erika, and Judy Yung. *Angel Island: Immigrant Gateway to America*. New York: Oxford Univ. Press, 2012. 69

Takahashi, photographed every inch of the walls with the poems on them. Then, Asian-American Studies departments were told about the poems on Angel Island, and this led to the formation of the Angel Island Immigration Station Historical Advisory Committee. This organization was able to get a $250,000 state grant toward the restoration of the barracks, thereby preserving the poetry.[51]

The poems were extremely important because they offer a firsthand account of the Chinese immigrants' experiences. In these poems, readers can see how painful the experiences were for detainees who had left everything behind to come to a new country that treated them like prisoners. Once the poems were discovered, there was a move on the part of the Angel Island Historical Advisory Committee to try and get the buildings restored for historical research. The buildings were remodeled, and Angel Island was reopened as a historical site in 1983. Visitors could finally visit, see the poems on the walls for themselves, and better understand what the living quarters were like.

The mistreatment was especially hard because of how long the immigration cases would drag out. The resources that Chinese immigrants had were mostly Chinese-American organizations, as well as several law firms. There were many law firms devoted to Chinese clients specifically, and the more active ones were Joseph P. Fallon, George A. McGowan, Alfred L. Worley, and Oliver P. Stidger III. Stidger III had his practice specifically geared towards Chinese immigrants, with those clients making up 85% of his business. He also was the main lawyer for many Chinese organizations, such as The Chinese Chamber of Commerce and the Chinese Six Company. Stidger was not a fan of the discrimination that was present in immigration law, but his reputation was tarnished when he was indicted in a smuggling ring case in 1917. Stidger was indicted and not allowed to practice law on Angel Island again until 1921. When the new immigration law was passed in 1924, he was furious, asking whether the discrimination would ever stop unless every single person of Asian descent was driven from the island. He remained a major advocate for Chinese immigrants until his death in 1959.[52]

The discrimination was a huge problem even for Chinese people who had American citizenship, such as Chin Sing, who was not allowed back in the United States after a two-year absence. Even though he could speak English and knew everything he possibly could about his hometown in California, he did not have the correct certificate to prove he was a native because it had been burned in a fire. He also did not have any white witnesses to confirm his identity. Sing's lawyer had to search for two months to find witnesses, who then correctly identified him.[53]

---

[51] Yung, Judy. "A Bowlful of Tears: Chinese Women Immigrants." *Frontiers: A Journal of Women Studies* 2, no. 2, 52-55. Accessed May 19, 2019. https://www.jstor.org/stable/3346011. 55.

[52] Lee, Erika, and Judy Yung. *Angel Island: Immigrant Gateway to America.* New York: Oxford Univ. Press, 2012. 92

[53] Ibid.

He was finally allowed into the United States five months after his initial arrival at Angel Island.

The presence of lawyers was extremely important to Chinese immigrants being allowed entry at all. According to one report, in 1924, 76% of Chinese immigrants were rejected and hired an attorney, and out of these cases, only 39 of them would not be deported.[54] In a lot of instances, the treatment toward the immigrants who hired the attorneys was noted as unfair. The appeals process was extremely difficult for many immigrants since it was financially and emotionally demanding. When World War II started, some of the Chinese immigrants waiting for an appeal were stuck on Angel Island for 20 months.[55]

Japanese Immigrants' Experiences

For more than two centuries, Japanese people were banned from immigrating anywhere, and that only changed in 1854 mostly because it became harder to enforce once Japan opened up for international trading.[56] Under the Tokugawa shogunate, Japan had famously isolated itself from the rest of the world. The system was essentially one featuring a very powerful warlord whose bureaucracy ran the country and managed to keep the fractious nobles under firm control. The era began when Tokugawa Ieyasu, a leader who can only be described as a military and administrative genius, became shogun in 1603. In becoming the dominating figure in Japan, Ieyasu defeated other powerful warlords and brought peace to Japan after a prolonged and devastating period of war. The emperor granted him the title of *shogun*, an old title meaning approximately "generalissimo."

The shogun system ran Japan from 1603-1868, and the shogun as a position can best be viewed as a combination of warlord and regent, with the essentially captive Japanese emperor as powerless, but symbolic of Japanese culture. The shogun ruled some of the country and adroitly balanced the aristocratic clans that controlled the rest of the islands. The system has been described as feudal, but it actually was a supple and considerably more competent way of governing than existed in most of the rest of the world. The government may have been repressive, but the typical Japanese people in Tokugawa Japan were far better governed than many contemporary Europeans.

The Tokugawa bureaucracy established a rigid and hierarchical social structure, and Japan severely limited contact with the rest of the world, although it was not the total isolation sometimes presumed. The government was quite aware of what was happening in the rest of the world, and the Japanese left a window open to Europe, in the form of a small and highly restricted Dutch presence on an artificial island in Nagasaki harbor, a presence that lasted more than 200 years. Courtesy of the Dutch, the Japanese were aware of contemporary events in

---

[54] Ibid, 93

[55] Lee, Erika, and Judy Yung. *Angel Island: Immigrant Gateway to America.* New York: Oxford Univ. Press, 2012. 92-93

[56] Ibid114

Europe, along with the rest of the world, and they were also aware of scientific and technological progress, although whether this resulted in any practical applications is hard to establish.

There had been a European presence in Japan well before the establishment of the shogun system, resulting in a sizable number of Japanese becoming Catholic Christians, largely through the efforts of Portuguese missionaries. Portuguese and Spanish missionaries had been very active throughout Asia from the early 1500s, so the Japanese were quite aware of the animosity between Dutch Protestants and Iberian Catholics. Under the early shoguns, Christianity was repressed, mostly because the government feared that Christians might aid the Europeans to Japan's detriment. Jesuits, for example, had considerable influence at the Ming Chinese Emperor's court, and eventually, the repression resulted in a Christian rebellion called the Shimabara Rebellion (1637-1638), which was savagely put down. Large numbers of Christians were killed, and while a small Christian presence remained, it only survived underground.

The merits of the Tokugawa period are still debated by historians, but it kept the peace in Japan for 250 years and prevented the kind of European colonial adventures that bedeviled much of the rest of Asia. Japan famously abandoned guns as weapons, despite arguably having the world's largest number of gunners in the 1590s when it invaded Korea. Japan's central government remained formidable enough to deter European meddling, and European ships attempting to visit Japan were treated harshly.

The Japanese stayed out of the chaos in China as the Ming dynasty collapsed and the Manchu conquerors replaced the Ming dynasty with their own, the Qing, but on July 8, 1853 the American Commodore Matthew Perry led four U.S. Navy warships into Uraga Harbor near Edo (later renamed Tokyo), presenting the Japanese with a letter from President Millard Fillmore. The Japanese couldn't know they were at the end of their long withdrawal from the rest of the world, but they were quite aware that the conditions in China and in Asia generally were being forced to change. They were also certainly aware that the Americans, as a result of the Gold Rush, had made California a state (in 1852) and extended the United States to the Pacific coast. They were also aware that American ships dominated the Pacific whaling industry, and that they commonly sailed to China. Japan was further aware of the British and French colonial incursions into China, and they were looking across the Sea of Japan where the Russians were actively occupying territory that was uncomfortably close to Japan. Thus, the appearance of an American naval force would have been ominous.

It became painfully evident that if Japan was to avoid becoming another victim of European colonial expansion, the country would have to become powerful itself. Progressive forces managed to come together, and they overturned the Tokugawa Shogunate. They legitimized their movement by focusing on the emperor, and in 1867, the Japanese effectively restored the imperial throne to a position of influence it had not held for centuries.

In the process, it became possible for Japanese people to leave the country, and some of the earlier immigrants left Japan because they dreamed of making it rich in America, where the U.S. dollar was worth twice as much as the Japanese yen. Many who moved did so because they were left devastated after the Meiji Restoration, which modernized many industries quickly.[57]

While the Japanese experience was slightly different than the Chinese experience, it was still difficult for them to come to the United States. The Japanese government and the American government actively collaborated on the exclusionary laws that would limit Japanese immigration. Many Japanese people were extremely successful farmers, and this was a threat to many Americans in the farming industry. When the Chinese Exclusion Act passed, the Japanese government decided to try to limit the amount of lower class people who could immigrate to the United States.

At the same time, Japanese immigrants did not want to be grouped in with Chinese immigrants, and they worked extremely hard to learn English and converted to Christianity. There was an attempt at a Japanese exclusion act in 1900, with all three political parties in the 1900 election running on an anti-immigrant and exclusionary platform. In 1906, there was a governmental decree to take all Japanese students and put them in "Oriental specific"[58] schools, which outraged the Japanese government.

In order to give American exclusionists something that they wanted, Roosevelt issues a decree in 1907 that stopped Japanese laborers from entering the United States from Hawaii, Canada, and Mexico. He then intervened in the school segregation issue, and in return the Japanese government stopped issuing passports to laborers.[59] This pact is referred to as "The Gentleman's Agreement," one of the prime examples of how important class was when it came to who was allowed into and out of the country.

Once this agreement was brokered between the United States and Japan, immigration from Japan dropped from 9,544 in 1908 to 2,432 in 1909.[60] In 1924, a new immigration act would come into effect and put an end to Japanese immigration completely. Once the quotas went into effect, the only Japanese people who were allowed into the United State were picture brides, women who were married to husbands already living in the United States through an arranged marriage process. It was a great way to immigrate to America, and it was also a great way for men to not have to travel back to Japan in order to find the proper bride. Most of these women had never met their husbands, but some were rejoining them.[61] A lot of Christian organizations were against these arranged marriages, so the Japanese government changed the rules in order to mandate that brides had to live with their in-laws for six months before they applied for a

---

[57] Ibid
[58] Lee, Erika, and Judy Yung. *Angel Island: Immigrant Gateway to America*. New York: Oxford Univ. Press, 2012.
[59] Ibid 116
[60] ibid
[61] Daniels, Roger. "No Lamps Were Lit for Them." *No Lamps Were Lit for Them: Angel Island and the Historiography of Asian American Immigration* 17, no. 1, 3-18. Accessed May 29, 2019. https://www.jstor.org/stable/27502236. 4

passport.[62] Japanese immigration was also aided by organizations such as the JAA (The Japanese Association of America), which wrote guidebooks helping young women immigrate. They instructed them on how to carry themselves, dress, and act in order to not "disgrace" their country.[63]

While these picture brides had shorter stays than Chinese women, it was still a shocking and often terrifying experience for many. In the interview for the picture brides, women were asked many questions about the husband they were about to join in America. Japanese picture brides would meet their husbands in the inspection room because immigration officials had to make sure that they were the correct men. Most of them had never met their future partners before, so the brides were asked for copies of her husband's family registry, as well as a letter from the Japanese consulate that assured the husband was able to support his new wife in America. Thanks in part to these kinds of arrangements, fewer Japanese women were accused of prostitution than Chinese women.

In 1919, things became more complicated for picture brides when the Oriental Exclusion League formed in order to shut down Japanese immigration and ban all Asians from ever acquiring American citizenship. The picture bride immigration was halted altogether in 1920 – from that point forward, if men wanted to have their wives come to the United States through arranged marriages, they would have to travel back to Japan, which was often risky. If they returned to Japan, these men would often be conscripted into the Japanese army[64], or they could be barred from the United States once they tried to return.

After the 1924 Immigration Act went into effect, only temporary visitors and those who were already American citizens were allowed into the United States. Some of this was to the advantage of American-born Japanese children who had been sent back to Japan for schooling. If they returned and had their relatives waiting on the dock for them, they were not detained on Angel Island.

While Japanese immigrants were the second largest group to come to Angel Island after Chinese people, there are few stories of their stays in the barracks because their detainment was typically much shorter. None of the poems found on Angel Island are in Japanese, further proof that they were not generally subjected to much scrutiny.

Everything would change after the attack on Pearl Harbor in December 1941. Eventually, the Japanese people who had successfully immigrated were removed from their lives and placed in

---

[62] Lee, Erika, and Judy Yung. *Angel Island: Immigrant Gateway to America*. New York: Oxford Univ. Press, 2012. 117

[63] Lee, Erika, and Judy Yung. *Angel Island: Immigrant Gateway to America*. New York: Oxford Univ. Press, 2012. 119

[64] Lee, Erika, and Judy Yung. *Angel Island: Immigrant Gateway to America*. New York: Oxford Univ. Press, 2012. 133

internment camps, and many historians have made comparisons between Japanese internment camps and Angel Island's detainment practices. They were overcrowded, the detainees were held in barracks, and they were given poor food and poor living conditions.[65] Some of the Japanese picture brides who had come from Japan for a brand new start suddenly found themselves in these internment camps, which was definitely not what they expected.

South Asian Immigrants' Experiences

South Asian immigrants had an extremely hard time in the United States, mostly because by the time they started coming in large numbers, Chinese, Japanese, and Korean laborers had already been banned from immigrating. There were no laws that specifically outlawed South Asian immigrants, so their presence became controversial for the country.

In the early 20th century, South Asians had no explicit prohibitions on the books, so those fleeing British colonial practices in places like India headed for America. However, they were quickly banned from the United States by the Immigration Act of 1917, and in all, South Asians had the highest rejection rate of all immigrants coming to America.[66] Exclusionists were furious about South Asians' presence in the country, insisting that they were inferior and were "threats to the existing racial order."[67]

The media did not help South Asian immigrants either, as the newspapers sensationalized their role in society. Newspapers ran headlines such as "Hindy Cheap Labor" and "Menace to Prosperity of Coast." One paper wrote an article entitled, "Turn Back the Hindu Invasion."[68] All of this makes sense within the context of the time, since yellow journalism was extremely prevalent in this period. This kind of sensationalism created a massive backlash among Americans, who believed that people of Indian descent were harming the economy and taking jobs from Americans. In short order, South Asian immigrants were turned away, and at one point 181 out of 184 immigration applicants who were South Asian were denied.[69]

Unlike the Chinese, immigrants from India did not have strong organizations that could advocate for them on Angel Island. The Hindu population who came often said that their first stop would be the Sikh Temple in order to find work, but the temples were not active in hiring lawyers. As such, many of those who came from South Asia relied solely on their family networks for support.

Once the restrictions passed in 1917, the only South Asians let in were those who had wealthy

---

[65] Lee, Erika, and Judy Yung. *Angel Island: Immigrant Gateway to America*. New York: Oxford Univ. Press, 2012. 140

[66] Ibid. 147

[67] Lee, Erika, and Judy Yung. *Angel Island: Immigrant Gateway to America*. New York: Oxford Univ. Press, 2012. 149

[68] Ibid

[69] Ibid. 151

backgrounds or were highly educated, but after World War II, the attitude of the country as a whole towards South Asian immigration changed drastically. India became an important ally in the country's war efforts, and in 1946, the Luce-Celler Bill allowed South Asian immigrants back in, as well as the right to apply for naturalized citizenship.[70] This marked the end of the exclusionary era of the United States, but the damage that the racism had done already to the South Asian community was already permanent.

Korean Immigrants' Experiences

Korean immigrants arrived at Angel Island around the same time as South Asian immigrants. In 1913, six Korean men arrived on Angel Island. Korea was annexed by Japan in 1910, and the men who arrived claimed that they were not subjects of Japan or Korea since they left the country before the annexation happened. The Korean National Association (KNA) helped the men get into the country, and they were the first known case of Koreans immigrating in the early 20th century.

Over the next three decades, 1,000 Koreans would try to enter the United States, and while only a small amount of them immigrated, they were the most accepted out of the Asian groups entering the United States. Korean immigration was completely shut down in 1918 by the Japanese, but 541 refugee students and 115 picture brides came to the United States from Korea before the ban.

Koreans felt a lot of hostility in the United States thanks to the dual pressures of the occupying Japanese government back home and racist Americans. The Korean National Association was extremely active, and it often provided money to hire lawyers and help people get through the immigration process.

While there are no Korean poems on the wall, one poem was published in a Korean newspaper in 1929. The poem reads:

"Angel Island, Angel Island, all the people said,
So I thought it would be like heaven. Yet when the iron-gate locks with a clang—it feels like hell.
You, the masses of people who are wriggling in this steel barred-prison,
You have a home, you have a country.
So what is the reason for this sorrow?
It must be a hungry belly that causes this Karma."[71]

Korean picture brides were also common, and this was the only way Korean women could get

---

[70] ibid 174
[71] Lee, Erika, and Judy Yung. *Angel Island: Immigrant Gateway to America*. New York: Oxford Univ. Press, 2012. 1999.

into the United States from 1910-1930. These women ranged in age from 14-25, and they typically came from wealthy backgrounds or educated classes.

Non-Asian Groups

In 1910, there was an influx of Mexican immigrants who were detained on the island due to the Mexican revolution. All of the foreigners living in Mexico were dispelled, and those included the Chinese immigrants to Mexico as well. In the early twentieth century, many Guatemalans who were wealthy immigrated to the Untied States through Angel Island, and were able to gain entry with supporting letters from the Guatemalan consul general and the money shown in their bank accounts.[72]

The white European immigrants on Angel Island fared better than their Asian counterparts. There were Russian immigrants on Angel Island who supposedly were allowed to have visitors every day from 11:00 AM -2:00 PM.[73] This would never have been allowed for Asian immigrants, and was considered a privilege. One French Canadian family of four reported in an interview that they were thankful for the four months they had in detention, because it was much nicer than the time they would have spent in Canada during the winter working.[74] While overall those of non-Asian descent enjoyed a less harsh experience, there were still some claims on the part of European immigrants that showed inhumane conditions. In 1917, a newspaper reported that European men were herded like cattle into a hospital room with German immigrants. One polish immigrant, Wladmir Pruszyaski described being detained on Angel Island in 1919 as, "worse than the life in prison."[75]

There was also an influx of Jews who were fleeing from Russian and Nazi persecution throughout the twentieth century. Many Jews found their way to the west coast of the United States, because one of the main hubs they escaped to was Shanghai. While Angel Island had a number of immigrants from Australia, New Zealand, and Europe, having white skin was often a protection at this immigration station. The white immigrant experience is no where near as traumatic as the Asian one to the United States, as Asians had laws directly aimed at them and were often thought of as an inferior race.

The End of an Era

Angel Island was once almost completely lost when a fire broke out in the middle of the night on August 12th, 1940. All of the detainees were removed from the building, and then it took hours to put out the flames. Although it was an emergency, guards were still instructed to keep people segregated by race and gender. This shows just how strongly the culture of separation was

---

[72] Ibid. 51
[73] Ibid. 59
[74] Ibid.
[75] Ibid. 60

on Angel Island. Some of the buildings on Angel Island were destroyed from the fire, and once it was out only the hospital and detention buildings remained. A lot of records were destroyed during the fire, because they had been locked in a vault in the administration building. These were valuable, because they were supposed to be the historical first hand records that we would have in the future. The detainees were kept on Angel Island but were forced to stay in the quarantine station and the hospital. They were served their meals in the yard of the complex.

Angel Island was a POW holding facility from 1940-1945, directly after the fire that took place in 1940 which ended it's era as an immigration station. During World War II, Angel Island was home to German, Italian, and Japanese prisoners of war before they were transferred to inland camps. Its proximity to the Pacific Ocean and its isolation from the mainland made it a good choice for an army prison. When Germany surrendered, there were 277 German prisoners on the island.[76] This was a perfect place to hold prisoners of war, because there were already hospitals and prison like barracks. In addition to acting as a POW holding camp, it was also the point from which troops went to war. More than three-hundred thousand soldiers passed through Angel Island to go into the Pacific sector of the war.

In 1963, the island was turned into a California State Park, but it remained abandoned until there were plans to convert it into recreational use in 1968. The immigration buildings would have been destroyed without the work that went into preserving the poems, which resulted in the historical preservation of the immigration station as a whole Angel Island received landmark status in 1996, and the buildings were slowly restored one by one. The restoration of the buildings and the immigration station helped to legitimize the Chinese immigration story and struggle, and the restoration represented a way for many Chinese-Americans to take control of their own history.

The first floor of the barracks was available for public viewing in 1983, the same year the Angel Island Immigration Station Foundation was founded by Paul Chow.

In 1993, there was a national public awareness campaign calling attention to the island's history. A traveling exhibit by David Quan known as "Gateway to Gold Mountain"[77] began touring to expose the rest of the United States to the history of Angel Island. Once it received landmark status, David Quan argued that its landmark status now made Angel Island equal to Ellis Island. This was a huge milestone for Asian-Americans, as Angel Island was only the second site (the first being Manzanar, a Japanese internment camp) profoundly affecting Asian-Americans to receive landmark recognition. [78] It was designated an endangered historical site in

[76] Angel Island--World War Ii in the San Francisco Bay Area: A National Register of Historic Places Travel Itinerary https://www.nps.gov/nr/travel/wwIIbayarea/ang.htm.

[77] Lee, Erika, and Judy Yung. *Angel Island: Immigrant Gateway to America.* New York: Oxford Univ. Press, 2012.309

[78] Lee, Erika, and Judy Yung. *Angel Island: Immigrant Gateway to America.* New York: Oxford Univ. Press,

1999, which brought access to some federal funding for restoration. The museum on the island was opened in 2009, the year the full restoration was completed.

Angel Island's legacy remains important as America continues to struggle with the immigration debate, and today it can be visited by anyone who cares to understand how an island in San Francisco Bay could have a profound impact on millions of Americans and their ancestors.

Online Resources

Other books about 20th century American history by Charles River Editors

Other books about Angel Island on Amazon

Further Reading

A Teacher's Guide to Angel Island Immigration Station. Angel Island Association. P.O. Box 866, Tiburon, CA 94920. (415) 435-3522.

Angel Island Immigration Station Historical Advisory Committee. Report and Recommendations on Angel Island Immigration Station. San Francisco: 1976.

Bamford, Mary. Angel Island, the Ellis Island of the West. Chicago: Woman's American Baptist Home Mission Society, 1917.

Chetin, Helen. Angel Island Prisoner, 1927. Berkeley: New Seed Press, 1982.

Chow, Christopher & Yu, Connie Young. "Angel Island and Chinese Immigration." San Francisco Journal. June 30, July 21, August 4, 11, 18, 25, 1976; revised version, published April 25, 1979.

Freedman, Russell (2013). Angel Island: Gateway to Gold Mountain. Boston (MA): Clarion Books. ISBN 978-0-547-90378-1.

Fu, Chi Hao. "My Reception in America." Outlook. August 10, 1907, pp. 770-773.

Lai H.M. "Angel Island Immigration Station." Bridge Magazine. April, 1977, pp. 4-8.

Lai H.M. "The Chinese Experience at Angel Island." East West Chinese American Journal. February 11, 18, 25, 1976.

Lai H.M. "Island of the Immortals: Angel Island Immigration Station and the Chinese Immigrants." California History. Spring 1978, pp. 88-103.

Lai et. al. Island. San Francisco: HOC DOI (History of Chinese Detained on Island), 1980. Reprint University of Washinton Press, 1991.

Lim, Genny & Yung, Judy. "Our Parents Never Told Us." California Living, San Francisco Examiner & Chronicle. January 23, 1977, pp. 6-9.

Lim, Genny. Wings for Lai-Ho. San Francisco: East/West Publisher, 1982.

McCunn, Ruthanne Lum. Chinese American Portraits. San Francisco: Chronicle Books, 1988.

McCunn, Ruthanne Lum. An Illustrated History of the Chinese in America. . San Francisco: Design Enterprises, 1979.

McDonald, Marshall & Associates. Report and Recommendations on Angel Island. 1769-1966. Oakland: 1966.

Power, Keith. "The Ellis Island of the West." San Francisco Chronicle. November 25, 1974, p. 5.

Soennichsen, John (2005). Miwoks to Missiles. Tiburon, California: Angel Island Association.

Sun, Shirley. 7hree Generations of Chinese - East and West. Oakland Museum: 1973, pp. 27-29, 33.

Takaki, Ronald. Strangers from a Different Shore. Boston: Little Brown & Co., 1989.

US. Dept. of Commerce and Labor. Bureau of Immigration and Naturalization. Annual Report of the Commissioner General of Immigration for the Fiscal Year. . . 1910-1913.

US. Dept. of Labor. Annual Report of the Secretary of Labor, For the Fiscal Year. . . 1928-1947.

US. Dept. of Labor. Bureau of Immigration. Annual Report of the Commissioner General of Immigration, for the Fiscal Year. . . 1914-1933.

Wang, Ling-chi. "The Yee Version of Poems from the Chinese Immigration Station." Asian American Review. Berkeley: University of California, 1976, pp. 117-126.

Yu, Connie Young. "Rediscovered Voices: Chinese Immigrants and Angel Island." Amerasia Journal Vol. 4, No. 2, 1977, pp. 123-139.

Yu, Yao Pei. "The Treatment of the Chinese by the United States Immigration Service." Chinese Student. August, 1936.

Yung, Judy. "A Bowlful of Tears: Chinese Women Immigrants on Angel Island." Frontiers. Volume 2, No. 2, 1977, pp. 52-55.

Yung, Judy. Chinese Women of America. Seattle: University of Washington Press, 1986.

Yung, Judy. Unbound Feet: A Social History of Chinese Women in San Francisco. Berkeley: University of California Press

.

Free Books by Charles River Editors

We have brand new titles available for free most days of the week. To see which of our titles are currently free, click on this link.

Discounted Books by Charles River Editors

We have titles at a discount price of just 99 cents everyday. To see which of our titles are currently 99 cents, click on this link.

Printed in the USA
CPSIA information can be obtained
at www.ICGtesting.com
LVHW082118080624
782712LV00015B/1229